I0532075

SHE IS

VICTORIOUS

A 30-Day Devotional for Collegiate

Female Athletes

Lori Malone

SHE IS VICTORIOUS

Copyright © 2026 by Lori Malone

All rights reserved. No part of this book may be reproduced in any form or by any means—whether electronic, digital, mechanical, or otherwise—without permission in writing from the publisher, except by a reviewer, who may quote brief passages in a review.

Unless otherwise noted all Scripture is taken from the Holy Bible, New Living Translation, copyright © 1996, 2004, 2015 by Tyndale House Foundation. Used by permission of Tyndale House Publishers, Inc., Carol Stream, Illinois 60188. All rights reserved. Scripture quotations marked NIV are taken from the Holy Bible, New International Version®, NIV® Copyright ©1973, 1978, 1984, 2011 by Biblica, Inc.® Used by permission. All rights reserved worldwide. Scripture quotations marked ESV are taken from the ESV® Bible (The Holy Bible, English Standard Version®), © 2001 by Crossway, a publishing ministry of Good News Publishers. Scripture quotations marked NKJV are taken from the New King James Version®. Copyright © 1982 by Thomas Nelson. Used by permission. All rights reserved. Scripture quotations marked AMP are taken from the Amplified Bible (AMP) Copyright © 2015 by The Lockman Foundation, La Habra, CA 90631. All rights reserved.

Published by
Frontline Ministries
WWW.GOFRONTLINE.ORG

Library of Congress Control Number: Applied for

Paperback ISBN: 978-1-956033-22-9
Ebook ISBN: 978-1-956033-23-6

Printed in the United States of America

This devotional is dedicated to every collegiate female athlete who understands that winning doesn't come easily. She knows the hard work, commitment, sacrifice and relentless drive needed to compete at the highest level and win. I pray she digs deep in God's Word and uses this devotional to sharpen and strengthen her spirit for battle daily as she lives victoriously for Jesus!

This devotional is also dedicated to my Lord and Savior, Jesus Christ, who rescued me from total darkness and gave me new life! To my parents, Craig and Verna, for never giving up on me and daily interceding, showing how parents must cover their children in relentless prayer. To my husband, Matt, for being a trailblazer in doing hard and uncomfortable things, like writing a book. He inspired me to share what was already written on my heart from long ago.

Contents

Introduction

We've been taught as athletes that the game is just as much mental as it is physical. We can do many things to help take our game to the next level such as staying after practice to get more reps, watch film, and even pay for private lessons. Our physical game gets all the attention and yet we are acknowledging there is a missing piece to becoming an elite athlete: the mental side of the game. Coaches, players, and parents know the importance of this critical piece and yet it takes hard work and discipline to put this game-changer piece into practice.

This devotional is created to step-up your game by applying Biblical principles to your sport as well as your personal life. The Bible talks about renewing our minds daily in the book of Ephesians. When we begin to sit with God's Word, apply it, pray, and let it take root in our heart, we are exercising our spiritual muscle that ultimately benefits our entire life!

My hope is that as you dive in over the next thirty days, you can relate to many of these athletic experiences, be encouraged by His Word, and be reminded that you are victorious in Christ Jesus. We have the victory because of Him!

I added a journal space to each day, reminding you to take time to reflect, answer a question, and apply what you just read. There's something to be said about writing your thoughts down on paper. Don't skip this step! You will notice the "Confess + Connect with Jesus" after. This space is designed to lead you into a heart of worship, prayer, and submission to Jesus. Lay every burdening thought, unconfessed sin, and hopeful dream at his feet. Your prayers written down are simply one way to talk to Jesus, take captive your thoughts, and reflect on his faithfulness. I encourage you to walk through each step and as you do, you are creating a discipline, habit, a way of living that promises ultimate victory-eternal life in freedom. In Christ, you are victorious!

Day 1

Brain Battles & Biblical Breakthrough

Where is your head?

Did you know that the average person has sixty to eighty thousand thoughts per day? That's roughly three thousand thoughts per hour!

Can we just stop and thank God for creating us with such intricately fast and beautiful masterpieces? If a machine were to compute that many thoughts per hour every day it would smoke from exhaustion.

Our brain is not hurting for things to think about daily. Our minds wander, daydream, or maybe even worry. We don't give it a second thought. Whatever pops in our heads, off we go!

If you're anything like me, your head races with "what if" scenarios. I will act on those thoughts and behave out of stress, worry, fear, anxiousness, or even doubt. My body responds physically to stress and worry. I get sick. My shoulders are tense from holding it in. My stomach screams to go eat ice cream or fast food. The spiral is out of control! How did I end up here?

The Bible says:

> "You will keep in perfect peace those whose minds are steadfast, because they trust in you." (Isaiah 26:3 NIV)

> "We demolish arguments and every pretension that sets itself up against the knowledge of God, and we take captive every thought to make it obedient to Christ." (2 Corinthians 10:5 NIV)

> "Do not conform to the pattern of this world but be transformed by the renewing of your mind. Then you will be able to test and approve what God's will is— his good, pleasing and perfect will." (Romans 12:2 NIV)

I want peace. I want God's perfect will. I want to be able to demolish those negative thoughts. But how? The Bible says to take every thought captive and keep your mind steadfast, focused on Him. Renew your mind!

Do you trust Him?

Are you firmly standing on the truth of God's Word? Are you reading His words of life and letting it sink deep into your heart daily?

Let go and let God take control. Is it time to release some pressure? Boy, wouldn't that be nice! It's a different peace. Peace comes by releasing control. Let it go and give it to Him.

> *"Cast your anxieties on him because he cares for you."*
> — *1 Peter 5:7 NIV*

When you *renew* your mind in the Word, surrender your thoughts to God, and trust that He will take care of your every need, then you will find peace and renewed faith for your life, your future, and your relationships!

How awesome would it be to have three thousand positive and edifying thoughts every hour of the day? I honestly believe our outlook on life would be much more pleasant and our bodies would thank us for not adding an extra workload to it.

Journal Time

What narrative do you respond to in your head? Does it create unnecessary stress? Or is it positive?

Over the next twenty-four hours write down some of your three thousand thoughts and describe them below.

Confess + Connect with Jesus

Day 2

Chasing God-Sized Dreams

Never stop dreaming!

I know of young girls who dream of becoming elite athletes. When you ask them, "what do you want to be when you grow up," they respond, "I want to be a professional ball player."

Why do they want to be a professional athlete? Because they know *professional* means the BEST!

I love the joy and dreams children have when they are young, because they know *nothing* is impossible! And that truth is biblical!

In Luke chapter one, the angel of the Lord, Gabriel, told young Mary (who was not in an intimate relationship) that she would bear a son, not just any son but the Son of God! And in that same breath, he revealed to her that her very old cousin is pregnant as well! How can this be?! Next to impossible, right? A virgin girl and a very old lady will both become pregnant. Can you imagine? If you keep on reading, we find out that both of these promises came true.

"Jesus looked at them and said,
'With man this is impossible, but with
God all things are possible.'"
— *Matthew 19:26 NIV*

What we learn from reading Scripture is that God is revealing his almighty power and boundless love for his children. If you have placed your faith in Christ, that's you and me!

Do you have dreams you've tucked away since childhood? Are there any ideas or creative goals you wish to accomplish? Do not let fear or naysayers stamp out your dreams. God has good plans for your life, and he has placed beautiful and captivating dreams inside your heart for a reason. Just like young Mary and her older cousin, these dreams are set before us. Do not get overwhelmed by the mountain that you think you have to climb to get there. Keep your eyes focused on Jesus, the giver of all good things. Let him carry the heavy load of directing and opening doors for you. Follow his lead. Tune a listening ear to his voice. Seek him above all else. As you surrender, you release control of the outcome. Your faith grows as you trust him. Give room to those dreams and bring them to the feet of Jesus believing in his timing and his way.

Just as we read in Matthew, remember that with God, nothing is impossible! Take Him into the center of your dreams and let Him breathe life into your big goals. Lean on Him for strength, guidance, wisdom, and courage to take a bold step of faith into the unknown. He will light your path, guide you and direct you. Then watch him do the impossible in and through you!

Journal Time

What dreams have you hidden deep in your heart that need to be resurrected?

Our God is a big God, and He can do all things! What will you need to let go of in order to start walking by faith toward your dreams?

Confess + Connect with Jesus

Day 3

Stronger Than Stress

When you were younger, you might have run into a problem or a situation that little you couldn't figure out how to get yourself out of. Maybe you were faced with a problem that just frustrated you to the point you were beside yourself. Have you ever been on the brink of losing it or throwing a tantrum but then you remembered who can come to your rescue? Someone who is way smarter than you, can fix things, is a problem solver? This person has come to your aid more than once before and you just *know* they will help you through this mess you are in right now.

How old were you? Were you little? How about in your teens? Who is that person that jumped out in your mind just now? Maybe this person is your mom or dad, your big brother, or a grandmother. This person brings a sense of calm to your heart. You run to them knowing they will jump into your mess with you and bring you out of it safely. Your mind is at ease. You feel the nerves in your body calm down. Your muscles are relaxing, and you hand over your burden to this person to help solve your problem. Isn't that reassuring knowing you have someone you can count on in your moment of stress?

Maybe there is no one who comes to mind for you. You might have a hard time going back in your past because you have felt abandoned, forgotten, or left alone. I want you to know that there are coaches, teachers and community officers who might be crossing your path today who are ready to help you when you need a listening ear. Take the courageous first step and ask if they can help you. Above all, know that God is always listening and wants you to talk to him every day.

Did you know God wants to be that person you go to when you are stressed or have a big problem to be solved? He has the answers. He is your Rock. The one who you can call on any time of day. He is near, and He is listening to your heart's cry. All you have to do is *believe*.

"The Lord is close to the brokenhearted." (Psalms 34:18)

"Call to me and I will answer you" (Jeremiah 33:3 NIV)

God walks with you. He is your comfort. He is your peace. He is your safe place to run to. Just like that person you trust will help you out of your problem, God is our ultimate help. We just have to call on the name of the Lord! Pray that He will give you wisdom and guidance and peace to navigate through this storm and watch him flood your heart and mind with hope.

> "Everyone who calls on the name of the LORD will be saved." (Romans 10:13)

> "And the peace of God which surpasses all understanding will guard your heart and mind in Christ Jesus." (Philippians 4:7 NIV)

There is nothing too big for our God. There is no mess too great that we have made for ourselves. There is no mountain too high that we cannot pass through when we are walking with Him.

> "Nothing will be impossible with God." (Luke 1:37)

Just remember the next time you feel stress rise. Your body and muscles tense. Your mind starts to wander. You feel exhausted from overthinking. You feel hopeless.

STOP!

Remember: MY GOD IS BIGGER!

And watch Him flood you with an everlasting peace and love that melts away the stress inside. You will get through this; you are not alone. He is right there with you saying let Me carry this for you.

Journal Time

Who is someone you turn to, ask for advice from, when you are stuck or in trouble?

How has God shown Himself to be bigger than your problems?

Confess + Connect with Jesus

Day 4

Pressure to Perform

Athletics somehow does that to us. We practice and put pressure on ourselves to perform flawlessly. We are so hard on ourselves and expect perfection each play. Not to mention the consequences the team faces if we mess up! We don't want to make a mistake!

Fear can be a powerful grip if we allow it. It freezes us. Makes us immobile. Takes over our thoughts and causes us to play the "what if" game. It invokes doubt to the point where self-condemnation consumes us. It makes us think twice before acting. We fear the consequences if we fail. We feel safer if we do not even try at all.

Fear that robs us of freedom is lethal. It is not healthy and creeps in like the Enemy who wants to steal our joy.

What if you could experience your game without fear—let loose and sell out each day you practice and perform? There is a sense of freedom that washes over you and gives you permission to be fully you, unashamed and unapologetic! It's powerful, it's dynamic, it takes you to another level of confidence, knowing nothing can hold you down.

Doesn't that sound amazing? Do you want that?

What if I told you the key to freedom is *love*?

> "Such love has no fear, because perfect love expels all fear. If we are afraid, it is for fear of punishment, and this shows that we have not fully experienced his perfect love." (1 John 4:18)

Fear directly opposes Christ's love. Love dispels all fear. But not just any love—God's perfect love. When you understand the magnitude of this kind of selfless love, it breaks off any fear the Enemy has against you. Chains of fear are broken, lies of failure are silenced, and the inability to move forward is stopped, in the name of Jesus! All we have to do is receive His love. Let the words of truth sink deep into your heart, plant seeds of hope in good soil, and renew your mind in the Word of God. Open the Bible and see what God says about fear.

> "But God showed his great love for us by sending Christ to die for us while we were still sinners." (Romans 5:8)

> "The Spirit you received does not make you slaves, so that you live in fear again; rather, the Spirit you

received brought about your adoption to sonship.

And by him we cry, 'Abba, Father.'" (Romans 8:15 NIV)

When you chose Jesus, invited Him into your heart, confessed your sins and made Him Lord of your life, there is no reason to go back to being chained in fear. Christ died for us once and for all! It is finished! Hallelujah! There is freedom in living your life with Christ at the center.

Choose today to quit partnering with fear. Cast out any doubt or sin that allows fear to take a foothold over you. Speak over your mind and heart, say, "Today, I choose to walk in freedom through Christ Jesus. I am washed by the blood of the Lamb. His love casts out the fear in my life. I partner with the King of kings and refuse to let the Enemy steal my joy from here on out! My God is greater. My God is bigger. And my God loves me! Nothing can separate His great love from me because I am His!"

Believe it. Speak it. Let His love overwhelm you with gratitude and gratefulness. And watch your mind and heart become renewed by Him. You will be transformed into a new player and have newfound confidence, freedom, joy, and peace! An unstoppable you in life and in the game. Keep your eyes focused on Jesus and let His love cast out fear.

How does fear hinder your performance?

Sit and reflect on Christ's sacrificial love for you. How does His love propel you to freedom?

Confess + Connect with Jesus

Day 5

Never Hang Up the Phone

Do you remember your first middle school crush? How smitten were you? Did you look to find ways to pass each other notes in the hallway or hang out at lunch? Did you get butterflies just thinking about him?

Now think about your high school love. You probably were more serious about hanging out with him. Texts and phone calls were endless. Showers and deodorant were a must! Maybe you even planned a group hangout just so your parents wouldn't hound you with a million questions before you walked out the door.

You couldn't stop thinking about him. You wanted to be around him. You loved the way you felt when you were in his presence. He made you feel some sort of way. The more you got to know him, the more he piqued your curiosity. You wanted to know EVERYTHING about him; what he liked to eat, what was his favorite color, what were his interests and talents. Does he have any cute quirks or a silly personality that comes out when he lets his guard down. If you were like me, you wanted to know the

REAL person deep down. I wanted to know ALL about my boyfriend. He was interesting, special, attractive.

Do you ever wonder who God is?

I'm sure your curiosity has leaned in this direction at least once or twice. But how can we ever truly *know* who God is? I'm glad you asked! We can find who God is by reading His Word. He's given us a big love letter, and all we have to do is read it! Below are just a few attributes of who God is:

He is the Bread of Life.

He is Living Water.

He is Love.

He is the great Healer.

He is all-powerful.

He never changes.

He is our banner.

He is omniscient.

He is eternal.

He is Abba Father.

He is our Creator.

He is holy.

He is a just Judge.

And the list goes on!

As you start to turn the pages, you will see who God is in every story told in the Bible. But don't stop there!

Just like your high school sweetheart, the more you got to know Him, the more you will want to talk to Him. I mean, after all, didn't you want to know *everything* about your sweetheart? You found yourself communicating with him daily for *hours*!

Likewise, let me encourage you to NEVER HANG UP THE PHONE on God. Prayer is your lifeline. When you want to know someone or deepen your relationship with them, you have to get their attention.

The more you stay on the line, the closer you feel to Him. Talk to God throughout your day: as you brush your teeth in the morning, eating lunch, getting ready for practice, or studying for a test. He wants to hear all about your day. Tell Him how you feel. Share your thoughts or frustrations with life or people. Thank Him for the good things going on in your life or sweet surprises that fell in your lap this week. Share your dreams and goals with Him. Whatever floats through your mind, He is all ears!

But don't forget that a phone call is a two-way street. When you talk to God, He listens—and He talks back! Wouldn't that be boring if your lover came to you only when they wanted to talk but never let you say anything back to them? That would be frustrating! So take time to pause and allow the Lord to speak to you. He wants to show you His love in many different ways. He speaks through dreams and visions. He speaks through words of encouragement from friends and loved ones. He speaks through His Word, the Bible!

> "Be still, and know that I am God; I will be exalted
> among the nations, I will be exalted in the earth."
> (Psalm 46:10 NIV)

> "Ask me and I will tell you remarkable secrets you do
> not know about things to come." (Jeremiah 33:3)

> "I will instruct you and teach you in the way you
> should go; I will counsel you with my loving eye on
> you." (Psalm 32:8 NIV)

> "You will pray to him, and he will hear you, and you
> will fulfill your vows to him." (Job 22:27)

> "I am praying to you because I know you will answer,
> O God. Bend down and listen as I pray." (Psalm 17:6)

God is our one true love! His love for you is far greater than you can even imagine. Begin to pick up that phone each morning as you roll out of bed and brush your teeth. Talk to God throughout your day. He is your best friend and always wants to hear your voice. There is nothing too small for him to hear and respond to. Just remember to never hang up the phone.

Journal Time

Who is always on your recently called list on your phone?

What are two ways you can practice "never hanging up the phone" spiritually this week?

Confess + Connect with Jesus

Day 6

DMs with God

Worship can be given by the words we say and how we walk out our lives, how we live our daily life.

Who do you follow on YouTube? Instagram? Tik Tok? Snap?

Do you follow celebrities, pro sports teams, influencers, successful professionals in your field of study? Do you get drawn in by watching them day after day? Does social media entice you down a rabbit hole of entertainment and distraction. Do you long to be like the influencers and celebrities, to have what they put on display for you to see?

What do you post? Do you take pics of a modified version of you? Only the *best* pics, portraying an image to the world that you are "making it" and everyone loves you?

If you want to take a real look at what is influencing your heart, scroll through your socials. Look at the pictures you posted. Read your captions. Scroll through the comments. How do they make you feel?

The image you portray can be a window to your heart. Are you longing to be like the celebs? Are you trying to put yourself out there in a certain light? Are you longing for feedback that will give you that dopamine hit repeatedly?

Pause for a moment and ask yourself are there any idols in your life that you want to be like?

Often, we think of worship as something we do in church when we sing before the preacher gets up on stage and delivers a message. Yes, this is an act of worship. We use our voices and words we say to glorify the Lord. We say how holy He is and how thankful we are for all He has done in our lives. We lift up our hands and surrender our hearts to Him.

This is an act of worship. On Sunday.

What about the other six days? What captivates your heart during the week? What words come out of your mouth? Do you cut others down? Or do you edify? Do you seek to be in the spotlight every chance you get? Or do you seek to find someone who needs words of encouragement.

Your life is an act of worship.

God longs for your heart. He created you! He is our heavenly Father who loves us so much that He gave His only son, Jesus, to die for our sins. What other person on Earth would do that for you? Through Christ, we have been given new life! Eternity spent with Him! There is so much to be thankful for. When we mess up, He gives grace. When we don't deserve a second chance, He gives mercy. The Bible says, "The steadfast love of the LORD never ceases; his mercies never come to an end; they are new every morning; great is your faithfulness" (Lamentations 3:22–23 ESV). He is faithful to his children. That is reason enough to worship Him!

When we sit and think of all the ways God has been faithful in our lives, how can we not want to lift up our hands and be grateful? Worship is a posture we take in *how* we want to live out our lives on Earth. Do we understand how forgiving our God is? Can we comprehend the depth of His love for us? And when we pause and reflect on all of these blessings in our lives, we cannot help but be overwhelmed by Him and His goodness.

How do we say thank you?

Our voices! We can praise Him on Sundays but don't forget there are six other days in a week. We can live our lives in gratitude! When Jesus captivates your eyes and heart, you start to become more like Him. You walk out this life in a new way. You see this world differently. You see people different. You love different. And you create a life that emulates Christ in a new way!

What has captivated your eyes and heart? And whatever you choose to say and do seven days a week, three hundred and sixty-five days a year, reflects who you worship.

Pray:

> Lord, open my eyes to see you all around me. Help
> me to pause and reflect on my own life and show me
> how to live more like you. I want to reflect your love
> and walk each moment out in true WORSHIP to you
> and your alone. Forgive me when I've worshipped
> others or even myself. I choose to put you back on the
> throne of my life. Open my eyes and cultivate the soil
> of my heart in gratitude and love. In Jesus' name, Amen.

Journal Time

What do you give the majority of your time and attention to outside of your obligations?

How can you intentionally worship God this week, outside of church?

Confess + Connect with Jesus

Day 7

Holy Mess!

Are you built for perfection?

I know you've played with or against an athlete who hates losing. (Maybe it's you!) Have you ever noticed their attitude go down the drain? They call others out, they blame others for their own mistakes, they refuse to take ownership of a team loss. It's as if they are the only athlete on the planet who plays flawlessly every game.

Honestly, someone who thinks their toots don't stink could use a little dose of reality check. Everyone messes up! No one is perfect.

Imperfect people have been walking this Earth since the beginning of time, when sin entered this world. It's part of our human nature to mess up. Let's take a quick look at a group of people in the Bible called the Israelites. You will find that we all aren't so different.

The Israelites were led by a man named Moses. He led approximately six hundred thousand men (not including women and children) out of slavery in Egypt. As Moses led the people, their hearts were overjoyed to be free and going to a new promised land the Lord had shown Moses. But when the journey took some twists and turns, the Israelites grumbled and complained.

> "It would have been better for us to serve the Egyptians than to die in the desert!" (Exodus 14:10-12 NIV)

> "If only we had died by the LORD's hand in Egypt! There we sat around pots of meat and ate all the food we wanted." (Exodus 16:3 NIV)

> "Why did you bring us up out of Egypt? Are you trying to kill us, our children, and our livestock with thirst?" (Exodus 17:3)

Eventually, Moses died and Joshua, the next leader, continued to lead them into the promised land—finally!

All along the way, the Lord provided for the Israelites. It's quite a miraculous story. As you read the book of Exodus, you will see the ups and downs of this group of people. One minute they are singing their praises with thanksgiving, and the next minute they blame and despise their leader.

You may look at these Israelites and say, "if only they would have had a better attitude and kept their mouths shut, they would see there is a light at the end of the tunnel." Before we get too quick to judge the Israelites, how often do our attitudes mirror theirs?

We complain and point the finger at anyone but ourselves! Just like that athlete who hates losing, we too get caught up.

I believe God shared this story of the Israelites in the Bible to remind us that we all stray from being good humans. We mess up. We get attitudes. We place blame. And that's okay if we understand that God continually gives us grace to start over again. We can walk in humility toward that athlete who thinks their toots don't stink. We can show them love and forgiveness because we know God first gave it to us.

Journal Time

Who do you need to extend more grace to in your life?

When you walk in humility toward others, what does that look like for you?

Confess + Connect with Jesus

Day 8
Brush Your Teeth

Have you ever felt too tired to brush your teeth? You've had an exhausting, incredibly long, day. You're counting down the seconds to when you can lay your head on that pillow and pass out. It's time to put this day to rest.

We have all felt that, but did you know the secret to a successful life is to brush your teeth?

You heard me right!

I've heard it said that life is a series of habits. And if that's true, what habits have you added to your day-to-day life? Do these habits benefit your life in the long run? Or are they time suckers, stealing your life away? Maybe you need to take ten minutes to write down a list of your daily habits you have adopted over the years either subconsciously or consciously.

Now let's get back to brushing your teeth! Today's devotion is about self-discipline. I'm not a dental hygienist, nor am I here to condemn you for not brushing your teeth every day. What I want you to think about is your self-discipline—even in mundane, routine habits like brushing your teeth. We only get one set of teeth in our lives (after our baby teeth fall out, of course). It's up to you to take proper care of them. Brushing twice daily. Maybe you have a good routine in the morning: you get out of bed and go straight into the bathroom and get it done. Good for you!

Nighttime, however, is another story.

You don't have the energy or maybe you stayed up super late to meet a deadline. Or maybe traveling home with your team took longer than expected, and now you just need to get as much sleep as you can before the next day comes at you.

Every now and then, we let it slide. But take caution, the more you "let it slide," the easier it becomes to skip it each night. Are you able to take care of the small things in your life regardless of how you feel? Have you created good habits that will stand the test of time even when you really could just skip it for the sake of more sleep?

You see, the secret to a successful life is not found in wealth or status but in small and steady habits that go unnoticed by everyone but you and Jesus. You know when you are slipping or letting things slide more than normal. Cling tight to these foundational habits if they are helpful and healthy for your heart, your well-being and your spirit.

God sees you, even in the little things. When you might not think they make a significant difference, remember God honors those who walk with integrity. Live a life pleasing to Him, even when the world says you can settle or skip over things at school or not complete your workouts entirely when you say you did.

God honors a woman of integrity. Not allowing herself to be led by feelings and emotions that drag her down. But continue to stay the course and choose to remain faithful in the small mundane things.

> "One who is faithful in a very little is also faithful in much, and one who is dishonest in a very little is also dishonest in much.'" (Luke 16:10 ESV)

> "His master said to him, 'Well done, good and faithful servant. You have been faithful over a little; I will set you over much. Enter into the joy of your master.'" (Matthew 25:21 ESV)

Brush your teeth. Why? Because you are building a lasting foundation that won't be shaken by the throes of this world. Your healthy habits cannot be compromised. You know what is right to do, even when it's unpopular.

Brush your teeth.

In doing so, you will see the life you envisioned come to life in God's timing!

Journal Time

Are you creating a life of discipline with your daily habits? List some good habits you already have that will serve you well for your future.

God sees and honors the small habits you begin to create. What habits you would like to start implementing in your life today?

Confess + Connect with Jesus

Day 9

"I Can't, I Don't Have Time"

"I need more time!" Have you ever said that? Maybe you're taking too long on a math quiz. Or you are bombarded with college homework, but you have practice, and you need to eat dinner and take a shower. Maybe you are at work, and you have a deadline to make sure everything is in stock and organized before your boss arrives.

If we could buy more time, I probably would spend a good chunk of my money on it . . . daily! But the bottom line is that time does not stand still. We can never control the ticking clock. Life passes us by. College comes and goes in the blink of an eye. Four years seems like forever, but here you are standing on stage receiving your diploma and where did the time go?!

Time always seems like the enemy in our story. "If only we had more time" is our excuse. But honestly, when we take a look at time, we realize it is a gift. Time is precious. Time is short. The famous author Harvey Mackay said, "Time is free, but it's priceless. You cannot own it, but you can use it. You can't keep it, but you can spend it. Once you've lost it you can never get it back." It is more precious than money. You can always earn more money, but when time has passed it will never return. People say money can buy everything, but money can never buy more time. The Bible says, "For everything there is a season, a time for every activity under heaven" (Ecclesiastes 3:1). So, understand the value of time and use it wisely.

If time is a gift, how are you treating it? A gift is valuable. You make room for the gift in your life. You don't waste it. But how often do we look at time as a gift? We race through life in a big hurry. Often missing the moments that we can never get back.

Here's the takeaway: what is a priority in your life? What you choose to do, or not do, is your choice. So choose wisely.

I used to feel so overwhelmed with all the things I *had* to do. There was pressure at work to manage it all, responsibilities to my teammates and coaches to be the very best leader I could be at practices and in games, the weight of being a good mother at home, and then I needed time for self-care! Does a woman really know what self-care looks like? Let's be real!

Deadlines, multitasking, lack of sleep, and juggling my life came crashing down on my head, and eventually I broke. Mentally, physically, emotionally, and spiritually I was drained. Exhausted. Nothing left in my tank, so to speak. Have you ever felt like this?

I was spinning out of control, because everything had control of me. With the help of my dad and a business mentor, I learned that not everything is a priority and not everything has to be done immediately. I learned to categorize my tasks, my to-dos, and my responsibilities. Once I understood what my priorities were, I was able to take action, letting all the less important tasks fall to the bottom of the list. Eek! That was a hard one to sit with especially since I want to do it all.

I still have trouble navigating my life daily, and when I do, I reach out to my cousin who is my accountability partner. We talk about what is important, what my goals for the week are, and what healthy habits I want to implement each week. I'm setting boundaries around my time. Healthy boundaries!

Take inventory of your time this week. Write down what you do all day. Keep track in blocks of fifteen or thirty minutes. It will be hard at first, but this will let you see exactly what you spend your time doing each day. This will tell you what you value.

If your goal is to have a nice house or car in the future, are you setting aside money to save or are you spending your entire paycheck on things you don't need?

If you want to get better at your sport, how much time do you dedicate each week to working on your skills?

If you desire to grow closer to God, do you prioritize it? How much time do you spend reading the Bible and praying, gathering in small groups, and sharing what God is doing in your life?

Take an inventory of how you use your time. And that will tell you what you value. Time is a gift. Use it well. We all have twenty-four hours in a day. What you prioritize will reveal what you value in your life.

"For where your treasure is, there your heart will be also."
— *(Luke 12:34 NIV)*

Journal Time

How do you manage your time? Do you have a calendar or digital tools?

List a few priorities in your life that you want to make time for this week.

Confess + Connect with Jesus

Day 10

Leadership 101

Do you consider yourself a leader?

I always wanted to lead. I'm the youngest sibling, the loudest, the most opinionated, and the most outgoing. I guess you could say I was born to lead. But did I consider myself a good leader in my college days? No.

Organized sports forces you to take a hard look at your own qualities. It's impossible not to compare yourself to your peers or even the next-level athletes. What I thought made up a good leader is someone who always says the right thing. A motivator. Someone who always makes the play. Someone who can put the team on their shoulders and carry it to victory. Someone we can rely on. But I was wrong.

My perspective of a leader automatically removed myself from this category. I am the hardest on myself. I doubt my capabilities. I don't stand out from the crowd. I am not a motivator. I don't know what to say in tough moments. Therefore, I must not be a leader.

What I wish I could have told my younger self was: that is a lie! I am a leader!

Even if you cannot relate to my experiences, know that you are a leader. We are all leaders!

When you think of a good leader who pops in your head? Maybe a sports figure, business guru, or spiritual mentor immediately came to mind. Someone wealthy, or making bold moves that gain the attention of the media.

Yes, these people may have qualities of a great leader, but did you know they didn't start that way? Every good leader had to build something out of nothing.

Pause for a moment and list five qualities of a great leader:

1._____

2._____

3._____

4._____

5._____

Take a look at yourself in the light of these qualities. Do you possess any of these qualities already? Are they already part of your everyday life? If so, that's amazing! Give yourself credit. You are leading yourself already!

Now I know there are some qualities that may be a little tougher to create as a habit in your life. I have my weaknesses, too. Don't let that sideline you from becoming the leader God put inside you. Did you know you were born to lead?

You have God-given gifts and talents. You can use them to help you become the leader you were called to be. Just because you might not have a team to rally or a group that follows you does not mean you are not a leader.

Before you ever have an opportunity to lead a crowd, you first must be able to lead yourself. Do you have self-control? Are you able to create good habits that spur on your goals and dreams? Do you have a good work ethic? Do you push through adversity when life knocks you down? Is your self-talk positive or negative? Do you have accountability with coaches and mentors who are full of wisdom and truth? All of these qualities can catapult you into a new level of leadership.

If you can work on leading yourself, you will naturally set an example for others to follow. No need to yell, scream, or carry the weight of the world on your shoulders just so you can be called a good leader. Begin with *you* and let God do the rest!

Journal Time

Who have you seen good leadership qualities from in your life? What did that look like?

What is one habit that I can focus on this week to begin leading myself better?

Confess + Connect with Jesus

Day 11

Get Rid of Toxins

Did you know toxic chemicals are everywhere? Some come from the environment while others are consumed without even knowing it. That's why it is imperative to pay attention to what is going on around you and how it affects your body. Don't live blindly, but desire to learn and grow in many areas of life.

Toxins can affect the body in a variety of ways. They can disrupt your gut health, digestion, nervous system, ability to focus, and your immune system's defense, just to name a few. Toxins can completely disrupt your entire system! Isn't it interesting that we don't *look* for toxins to ingest, but somehow they creep in from all angles if we don't pay attention.

Slowly, our bodies shut down on us, and we don't know why. It's not an immediate response, and all too often it goes unnoticed. We feel sick, something is off, or maybe even a trip to the ER becomes necessary.

Just as physical toxins can negatively affect our bodies, spiritual and emotional toxins can block or impair our spiritual health too. We want to be healthy; we want to bear good fruit in our lives. We all do!

So what toxins have you let infect your heart, mind, and spirit? What spiritual and emotional toxins do you need to be rid of to function at your optimal potential?

How do we get rid of spiritual toxins? Let's look at the following scriptures:

> "Understand this, my dear brothers and sisters: You must all be quick to listen, slow to speak, and slow to get angry. Human anger does not produce the righteousness God desires. So get rid of all the filth and evil in your lives, and humbly accept the word God has planted in your hearts, for it has the power to save your souls." (James 1:19)

> "It is what comes from inside that defiles you. For from within, out of a person's heart, come evil thoughts, sexual immorality, theft, murder, adultery, greed, wickedness, deceit, lustful desires, envy, slander, pride, and foolishness. All these vile things come from within; they are what defile you." (Mark 7:20–23)

"Since you have heard about Jesus and have learned the truth that comes from him, throw off your old sinful nature and your former way of life, which is corrupted by lust and deception. Instead, let the Spirit renew your thoughts and attitudes. Put on your new nature, created to be like God—truly righteous and holy." (Ephesians 4:21–24)

"So stop telling lies. Let us tell our neighbors the truth, for we are all parts of the same body. And 'don't sin by letting anger control you.' Don't let the sun go down while you are still angry, for anger gives a foothold to the devil. If you are a thief, quit stealing. Instead, use your hands for good hard work, and then give generously to others in need. Don't use foul or abusive language. Let everything you say be good and helpful, so that your words will be an encouragement to those who hear them." (Ephesians 4:25–29)

"Get rid of all bitterness, rage, anger, harsh words, and slander, as well as all types of evil behavior. Instead, be kind to each other, tenderhearted, forgiving one another, just as God through Christ has forgiven you." (Ephesians 4:31–32)

The Bible is full of instruction and wisdom! These are just a few verses, and there is so much we can take away from each one; it will take a while to address all of the toxins that are identified.

Whatever the Lord lovingly convicts you of, I encourage you to sit with it. Surrender it daily in prayer, and ask Him for help in getting rid of these toxins in your life.

We all want to be physically healthy, but most importantly, God wants you to have a healthy spiritual life too. This is where true life springs from, your heart. When you work on your heart, you will be able to hear God clearly, resist the lies that the Enemy tries to get you to believe, and you will walk in true freedom.

"But you belong to God, my dear children. You have already won a victory over those people, because the Spirit who lives in you is greater than the spirit who lives in the world."

— 1 John 4:4

What toxin does the Holy Spirit want to help you gain victory over this week?

How does your mind and body respond to toxins in your life?

Confess + Connect with Jesus

Day 12

The Lioness Within You

Do you have grit? Do you have drive, determination, endurance, self-control, and that competitive edge?

Can you keep your head on straight when your emotions are running high? Can you separate the noise from the goal in front of you? Are you willing to sacrifice the good things of this life for the best thing that you really want to go after? Do you bounce back from failure with an even more determined mindset? Can you boldly choose the narrow path to walk down when you are faced with a fork in the road? Are you a woman who refuses to back down? Can you win the battle in your mind when you are faced with compromise?

These are just a few character traits any athlete wants in order to achieve their highest goals and dreams. If I could sum up these characteristics in one animal, it would be *lioness*.

Did you know lionesses are the hunters of their pack? They can take down animals twice their size. Talk about a superpower!

That's incredible! Lionesses are also leaders within the pack; they are confident and decisive. They are selfless and sometimes do not even get to eat their spoils because they allow the males to feast first. Lionesses are team players; they work together in so many ways to survive and thrive. They teach and protect their young. They are symbols of servant leadership, strength, and love. If you ever get a chance, read up on lionesses. They are incredible creatures and display many godly traits I believe every woman is called to possess.

You are an athlete! You possess qualities that are unique and set you apart from the rest. Don't let your fears or weaknesses stamp out the lioness that is emerging inside of you!

"The wicked run away when no one is chasing them, but the godly are as bold as lions."

— *Proverbs 28:1*

Journal Time

What fierce qualities of a lioness do you possess?

What is one trait you can learn from the lioness?

Confess + Connect with Jesus

Day 13

When Progress Feels Like Setbacks

Have you ever found yourself thinking: *Life is just not going the way I had envisioned*? Or maybe it has taken you to a place that was unexpected. Or maybe you are still waiting. Frustration is taking its toll on you, and you've just about had enough.

Friend, I've been there. It's taken me almost a decade to learn this lesson and find joy in the journey.

I cannot create a formula to magically get you to the place where you want to be. I know it's frustrating. You just want to get out of this. But let me offer a new perspective, if you are willing to listen.

There is a way out! But the path we often are called to take is a tough one. Jesus had an end goal: to save His people from eternal destruction, but that meant He had to make the ultimate sacrifice: laying down Hs life in our place. The perfect Lamb of God shed His perfect blood for you and me so that we can live eternally with Him in Heaven one day. That sounds amazing! But the way to eternal life was through the cross. Jesus had to endure the most brutal pain and suffering for our freedom.

Did he want it to stop? Yes, I'm sure! Was the journey to the cross a joyful one full of happiness and simplicity? No. But Jesus kept the vision. He walked this Earth knowing He was walking toward this pinnacle moment of suffering and death. But here's the lesson: He was filled with compassion, love, and yes, even joy, knowing the end is our reward.

> "We do this by keeping our eyes on Jesus, the
> champion who initiates and perfects our faith.
> Because of the joy awaiting him, he endured the cross,
> disregarding its shame. Now he is seated in the place
> of honor beside God's throne." (Hebrews 12:2)

Now it's your turn. Even in the waiting, in the middle of patience running thin, and in the midst of unmet expectations, you can find joy, peace, and longsuffering. Can you walk with a renewed sense of peace knowing God is growing your faith even in the frustration?

> "Father, if you are willing, please take this cup of
> suffering away from me. Yet I want your will to be
> done, not mine." (Luke 22:42)

Can you hear Jesus' cry to the Father? The pain He was about to endure was heavy. He knew it. But He was willing to walk this assignment out to completion. You can find joy in knowing the result. But what do we do when we have no end in sight? You place your faith in the One who created you with a purpose.

Set your focus not simply on reaching the light at the end of this tunnel, but open your eyes to what is around you right now and find joy in the journey.

So, get out a journal, a pen, and sit in a comfy chair or even go to a park surrounded by nature. Begin to pour out your heart to God. Tell him your frustrations, your expectations, the emotions that come with it. Let it all out.

And then look around you. Take a deep breath and follow Jesus' example.

Not my will, but yours be done.

If part of your journey includes the waiting, then you must embrace this season of your life with patient expectation and joy.

After looking around you, list some things you are grateful for. What blessings have you already experienced up until now? Where have you seen God show up in your life? Maybe it's in the small things. There's no blessing too small to be thankful for!

Have you lost your attitude of gratitude? Maybe it's disappeared and been replaced with anger or frustration or even fear. Make the choice to be thankful and you will see your heart change. Just like a muscle you work out in the gym, flex that gratitude muscle daily!

The more you do it, the bigger it will become. Pretty soon you will have new eyes to see the gifts God has given you for today and a fresh hope for tomorrow. He's got you! He sees you! And watch Him do a good work in you while you wait.

Journal Time

Do you feel like your life is at a standstill or even going backwards? Why is the season of waiting so hard?

Take a moment to close your eyes and think of a few things you can be grateful for today. Don't skip over this quickly! Give pause to your life in this season and reminisce on Jesus' faithfulness.

Confess + Connect with Jesus

Day 14

Who's Your Coach?

Accountability is what keeps you focused, humble, honest, motivated, and often full of integrity.

For me, there are a few people who I am accountable to in certain areas. My husband. He sees every part of me. My life, my habits, my actions and my words. When I say something, I must follow through because our family dynamic rides on our decisions. He sees my weaknesses and knows my strengths and sharpens me every day.

Our advisory board for our ministry holds us accountable to the budget, keeps us grounded in our vision, and covers our backs when we miss something. They are hands-on in our ministry and encourage us as we link arms and put our heads together to propel the ministry forward.

My cousin and I hold a weekly accountability meeting on Mondays. We check in and discuss the tasks for the week and label them as most important all the way down to self-care and exercise. Organization is important for me to be able to function throughout the rhythms of our life.

I lead weekly Bible studies with my college girls and they help keep me accountable to my time in the Word. It is imperative to grab a few friends and dive into the Word together. When we pick a devotional, a Bible reading plan, or pick a study topic to help guide us, it spurs on conversation, and we can see God move. We share stories, we ask questions, we encourage one another, and we pray together. Our faith begins to grow, and we have a place to share our hearts.

> "For where two or three gather in My name, there am I with them." (Matthew 18:20 NIV)

> "Without wise leadership, a nation falls; there is safety in having many advisers." (Proverbs 11:14)

Just like a coach holds athletes accountable and pushes you to be and do your best, we must surround ourselves with wise influences and mentors in all areas of life. Who you cling to will determine the direction of your path in life.

The ultimate Head Coach is our heavenly Father. He guides, directs, sharpens, encourages, uplifts, walks alongside, carries the load for us, and goes before us. He is always with you! Will you allow Him to be your Coach? Will you willingly allow Him to mold and shape your life into something beautiful beyond your imagination?

It requires laying down the crown of control and surrendering to His better and perfect will. Will you choose to open up your heart, surrender to Him and place your faith in His mighty hands? If you have not asked Jesus to be the Lord and Savior of your life, I would be honored to walk you through a simple prayer of salvation at the conclusion of this book. When you move into the passenger seat and let God take the wheel of your life, He will be your true Coach who is for you and loves you and will take you to a new level of freedom you never thought possible. Don't live your life alone! There is power and freedom in accountability, and you will be a better athlete and female for life.

Journal Time

What areas of your life do you value the most? (Romantic relationships, spiritual walk, finances, academics, social life)

How do you have accountability in these areas?

How will accountability propel you or keep you on the right track rather than doing it alone?

Confess + Connect with Jesus

Day 15

Not Enough + Still on the Team

I can remember not too long ago, trying my hand at a new sport. I've said goodbye to my athletic college days long ago, but nonetheless I wanted to try a new hobby: pickleball. It's like tennis meets Ping Pong. I thought, "How hard can this be?" Once I got the hang of it, I was hooked—like the millions of other pickleballers around the world!

I even convinced my husband to sign up with me for a local tournament to try winning at least the bronze medal. After all, we both are super competitive, athletic, and love a good rally. I had been focused for months on getting better at this game. I played multiple matches a week for hours on end. I couldn't stop. I wanted to work on my weaknesses and beat everyone I could. I watched film by myself, learned new tips and tricks from other professionals in this game, and found pro pickleball matches on ESPN. I must have talked about it so much to everyone that AI caught on and my social media feeds were flooded with videos of everything related to pickleball. I took the bait, hook, line, and sinker! You could say I was a little obsessed. I dreamed about my form and placement of my shots on the court.

It was tournament day. I could barely sleep the night before. I packed my protein snacks and hydration stick. I brought two paddles just in case I broke one. *Seriously?* Yes. I'm dead serious. We sized up the competition, and we concluded we totally could beat them. There were only seven teams in our division. We should be top three or four.

The first game—we lost. Then we came back and won the next one. Then we lost. And lost again and again. We were one for five. Wow! How did that happen?! I was shocked at our complete failure. I was angry, embarrassed and wanted to play again. But the bottom three teams had to go home. So, with our bags packed and tails tucked between our legs, we got in the car. I felt like a loser.

Have you experienced something like this defeat? You had practiced all year long and even came in and took extra reps. You watched yourself on film, met with the coaches and got feedback. You worked hard! You stayed focused on getting better. To win. To earn that spot on the field. And for some reason you failed. Repeatedly. You came up short where you had felt so prepared. It's frustrating! Blindsiding, to be honest.

What do you do when all you have isn't good enough?

After I licked my wounds, I reflected. I know I worked hard. I am proud of the way I pursued a goal. I stretched myself, learned, and became more knowledgeable about my newfound sport. I asked for help. All these things showed me that I can overcome obstacles.

I learned that what I choose to focus on is crucial!

My self-talk can help me or harm me. I can be so hard on myself for not achieving greatness like I had planned. My thoughts become negative, and this pattern of thinking has led me down some dark paths in my life. So today, I chose to preserve my good thoughts and renew my mind on what is true. I opened my Bible to remind myself of all the truths that God says I am, such as:

> "His grace is all you need." (2 Corinthians 12:9)

> "Remain in me, and I will remain in you. For a branch cannot produce fruit if it is severed from the vine, and you cannot be fruitful unless you remain in me." (John 15:4)

> "Think about the things of heaven, not the things of earth." (Colossians 3:2)

> "You will keep in perfect peace all who trust in you, all whose thoughts are fixed on you!" (Isaiah 26:3)

"You are a chosen people. You are royal priests,[a] a
holy nation, God's very own possession." (1 Peter 2:9)

"So if the Son sets you free, you are truly free." (John 8:36)

"For God has not given us a spirit of fear and
timidity, but of power, love, and self-discipline."
(2 Timothy 1:7)

"You are the light of the world—like a city on a
hilltop that cannot be hidden." (Matthew 5:14)

"See how very much our Father loves us, for he calls
us his children, and that is what we are! But the
people who belong to this world don't recognize that
we are God's children because they don't know him."
(1 John 3:1)

I am free, forgiven, chosen, set apart, loved, called to be a light, a
child of God, strong, and courageous. All these verses remind me
who I am. My identity is in Christ, and He knows my worth is
not tied to my successes or failures. By His grace I will get back
up and keep on working hard because He gives me purpose in
this life! My purpose is found in Him, and no one can take that
away.

Oh, and I'm still not done! I am determined to do better at my next tournament. In the meantime, I will remind myself that I am enough because He is all that I need!

Journal Time

What is something you pursued and fell short of your goal?

How do you handle disappointment?

When you feel insufficient, what is a good reminder that Jesus is all you need?

Confess + Connect with Jesus

Day 16

Four Tips to Going Pro

Don't you want to be the very best at your sport?

Dominate, compete and repeat!

Every true athlete desires to be successful. But what does it take to be the top dog?

I've heard it said that ten thousand hours of training will do the trick. I believe there is more to it than simply logging your hours, though. There must be a focus. There is a significant difference in "throwing the ball around" for two hours and a goal-oriented practice. Wouldn't you agree?

If you want to go pro, consider these four tips:

> **Prioritize your sport** – You have 168 hours to use each week. How much time will you set aside to dedicate to getting better?

Create a plan – Plan your skill work, drill work, strength training and flexibility. Make time for the film room, competition, and feedback.

Have a mentor – Seek out a mentor or coach who you trust who will guide you, hold you accountable, and push you to your highest potential.

Inner motivation – Determine to let go of everything else that does not benefit your main focus. Choose to not be distracted by every little thing and you will start to create good habits. Can you be consistent over time? How do you handle adversity? How bad do you want this? Are you in tune with your body? Can you self-reflect and regroup?

Have you ever noticed professional athletes who prepare for the Olympics only want to train with the highest-level peers? Why? Because they want to be the best! You must compete with the best to challenge yourself. That's what pushes you to become better.

Do you know someone who only likes to compete with lesser talent just so they can win? Or maybe they fudge their skills or rankings, so they can dominate in the lesser division. We all know that this does not make them a high caliber athlete. Instead, it says much more about their character than their talent.

Wise athletes risk the comfort of their pride for a greater gain in the end. Surround yourself with like-minded athletes with high level skills, and you will naturally rise to the occasion of competition! "As iron sharpens iron, so a friend sharpens a friend" (Proverbs 27:17).

Likewise, in your spiritual walk, if you desire to grow closer to the Lord and know Him better, you can apply the 4 tips above. God says, "If you look for me wholeheartedly, you will find me" (Jeremiah 29:13). Because you prioritize God within the hours of your week, He sees this and promises to bless you. It's like the game hide-and-seek or Where's Waldo? You must look high and low. Take your time to uncover all corners and look in places that seem unassuming. When you focus on one thing—God—He will make himself known to you!

"You will seek me and find me when you seek me with all of your heart." (Jeremiah 29:13 NIV)

Surround yourself with people who exhibit attitudes and behaviors that you would like to mimic. Maybe you want to be more joyful, patient, kind, or have better self-control. Think about who you know and start inviting them into your daily life! They are the ones who will sharpen you in life. Get to know them better. Take them out to lunch, ask them to share their story with you. Let them know you admire these qualities in them.

As you sit with the Lord, pray, read His Word, and reflect on your daily life habits, He will draw near to you. Remain in His Word and be faithful with your time spent with Him. I promise, you will see changes happen! Only good can come from sitting with the Lord daily and meditating on His Word. The more hours you devote to Him, surround yourself with like-minded people, stay persistent and stay focused on Him, the more you will see your faith rise to new levels.

Journal Time

What is one priority for you as a student athlete this year?

What area do you need to focus on to dominate in your sport?

How much time do you spend practicing for competition? How much time do you spend pressing into Jesus?

Confess + Connect with Jesus

Day 17

Unplugged and Unaware

Have you ever been vacuuming a large room and the plug accidentally disconnected because you went too far? What happens? The vacuum turns itself off. The chord didn't allow you to go as far as you hoped it would. Isn't that the worst? You're *almost* done and . . . BAM! Now, you have to go find another outlet.

Now hang with me. If we are the vacuum just moving along in life, going back and forth through each day—cleaning up, working, gym time, studying, and social life—minding our own business, then all of a sudden, WHAM! Something unpleasant happens and life comes to a halt.

You wonder, "How did I end up in this mess?"

Or "Why is life so unbearable right now?"

When I find myself in these predicaments, I scratch my head and wonder, *What is happening?* Maybe you can relate. It's as if the world stops spinning. My emotions are out of control. Maybe it's simply that things just feel off. What do you do?

I can remember one time trying to solve my own problems, do all the brainwork possible to get back on track. But it wasn't helping. Then I prayed. I put down the busyness of my brain and was just quiet before the Lord. I was still. It was literally that afternoon that I got a word from God, an image of a vineyard and then this verse:

> "Remain in me, and I will remain in you. For a branch cannot produce fruit if it is severed from the vine, and you cannot be fruitful unless you remain in me. Yes, I am the vine; you are the branches. Those who remain in me, and I in them, will produce much fruit. For apart from me you can do nothing." (John 15:4-5)

Wow! Thank you, Jesus! This verse was exactly what I needed to hear for my heart and my mind.

Now, let's go back to the vacuum.

Imagine you are the vacuum, and something causes you to randomly shut down, forces you to stop what you are doing. Isn't life like that sometimes? Sometimes it stops you in your tracks! What did I do? I had to go back to the power source because the vacuum was *unplugged!*

Who is the power source?

God!

I needed to plug back in to His power! I had wandered so far
from Him in my day-to-day life that my chord just would not
stretch any farther. Sometimes to wander isn't necessarily bad. It
could just mean you're distracted, letting your emotions take
control, or simply focusing on the problems and forgetting Jesus
is your Rock. He is our power source. We cannot forget that He
is our source of life and life abundantly.

Stay plugged in to Jesus, and He will give you the supernatural
power to face all that life can throw your way! He is your source
of life. Without Him, we can do nothing.

Journal Time

What does being "plugged in" to the Source look like for you?

What happens in your life when you are unplugged?

Confess + Connect with Jesus

Day 18

Where Is Your Superpower?

Do you have a favorite superhero? Maybe you loved watching them in cartoons or movies. I remember in elementary school being asked, "Who is your favorite superhero?" I unashamedly replied, "Mighty Mouse!" I could relate to this character because I was small, but I liked to think I was *mighty*.

Nowadays, Hollywood has created a superhero of every shape, size, ethnicity, superpower, and the list goes on.

People are fascinated with supernatural things. Filmmakers create entire worlds on planets that don't exist. Epic battles ensue. Just when we think there's no way out, the superhero comes just in time to save the day!

The same goes with our spiritual walk.

We were created to live supernaturally. God created us as spiritual beings. When we understand our purpose and calling here on Earth, we realize that we cannot function without His supernatural power!

"But you will receive power when the Holy Spirit comes upon you. And you will be my witnesses, telling people about me everywhere—in Jerusalem, throughout Judea, in Samaria, and to the ends of the earth." (Acts 1:8)

For God did not give us a spirit of timidity or cowardice or fear, but [He has given us a spirit] of power and of love and of sound judgment and personal discipline [abilities that result in a calm, well-balanced mind and self-control]. (2 Timothy 1:7 AMP)

"Put on the full armor of God, so that you can take your stand against all strategies of the devil. For we are not fighting against flesh-and-blood enemies, but against the evil rulers and authorities of the unseen world, against mighty powers in this dark world, and against evil spirits in the heavenly places." (Ephesians 6:11–12)

"We are human, but we don't wage war as humans do. We use God's mighty weapons, not worldly weapons, to knock down the strongholds of human reasoning and to destroy false arguments." (2 Corinthians 10:3–4)

God has created us to live supernaturally. Did you know this? It is only by his Holy Spirit that we can have the power and boldness to walk in the fullness of God. There are spiritual weapons that He gives us to fight the Enemy. If we choose not to walk in that supernatural power, we forfeit our God-given right to live a victorious life. We would be bound by our circumstances, chained by our hopelessness, and defeated by our insecurities. It's like going up to the plate without your bat in hand. We cannot walk into battle without our weapons; we are guaranteed a defeat!

Grab the Word of God and read His game plan! We have all we need to live a supernatural life through Christ Jesus. Read the Bible as his instruction book for direction, correction, and the ultimate victory. God has uniquely gifted us with his supernatural power, so we can live and do what He has called us to do. Don't waste the gift and simply live life in your own power. Tap into His supernatural power and see God show up in ways you never dreamed possible and consider these verses as you go about your day:

> "Don't copy the behavior and customs of this world but let God transform you into a new person by changing the way you think. Then you will learn to know God's will for you, which is good and pleasing and perfect." (Romans 12:2)

> "Therefore, since we are surrounded by such a great cloud of witnesses to the life of faith, let us strip off every weight that slows us down, especially the sin that so easily trips us up. And let us run with endurance the race God has set before us." (Hebrews 12:1)

Journal Time

How does knowing that you have supernatural weapons to fight your battles change your perspective on handling life's curveballs?

Read Ephesians 6. What are the weapons God gives us and how can you use them today?

Confess + Connect with Jesus

Day 19

God's Definition of a W

Go ahead and find a ruler. You know, the old school rulers that we used to bring with us to elementary school. If you don't have one, I've drawn one here, but holding a ruler in your hand is a great visual for this lesson.

If you could make a list that defines what success looks like to you, write them next to the ruler here.

Success means different things to different people. It all depends on the individual. If you've never thought about your own definition of success or greatness, now is a wonderful time to ponder.

You can define success as an athlete or as a female in general. Either one you choose (on or off the playing field), let's look at this ruler you have created.

We have just listed the ideals or characteristics of success. In our minds, if we achieve these things, then we are well on our way to being successful.

Sometimes, in the middle of me climbing my own ladder of success, I tend to peek over and see what others are doing. It's a natural response to want to compare. And comparison usually only makes me feel worse about myself. Ugh! Or I begin to judge others to make myself feel better about where I am on my own ladder. Ha! That sounds terrible, doesn't it? But it's true that the comparison trap can quickly spiral out of control.

Now here comes the plot twist.

What if I told you the problem was *not* in comparing your own success to others? The problem lies in what your *own* ideas of success is in the first place.

Have you ever stopped to consider how God defines greatness? What if we have it all wrong? Has His measurement ever crossed your mind? What does that even look like?

At a women's retreat in California the Lord opened my eyes to this concept as He spoke through the guest speaker for the night. We tend to compare ourselves favorably to others. "At least I'm not as bad as so and so." Or "I'm just as good as so and so." When in reality all human efforts fall infinitely short of divine perfection. The Bible describes our best righteousness as "filthy rags" before God (Isaiah 64:6). This chasm between the divine and human standard underscores our inability to earn salvation or justify ourselves through our own good works. Our salvation is found not in what we do but in the perfect righteousness of

Jesus Christ, which is offered to believers by grace through faith. God's standard is rooted in his absolute holiness and moral perfection, which is an unchanging and flawless measure of righteousness.

MIND. BLOWN.

My measurement of success was determined on *my* thoughts and *my* ideals. I never stopped to ask God what *His* measuring stick for greatness looked like. Up until that point in my life I had lived each day making choices that I thought were catapulting me toward greatness. Not once did I consider God's ideals. No wonder my life was not producing good fruit. I was barking up the wrong tree! Like a dog who chases a cat up a tree, I was the dog barking at the wrong tree while the cat was in another tree entirely. Wrong focus!

I had to pray. Seek the Lord. Open the Bible and read His words. Then I understood His measurement for greatness, and it looked so different than mine. Here are just a few of the criteria for success according to God's standard:

Humility

We need to know we are not as good as we think we are. Pride is directly opposite of Christ's teachings. Even some of the disciples struggled with this one. They were asking Jesus who was the greatest in the kingdom of Heaven.

"Anyone who wants to be first must be the very last, and the servant of all."— Mark 9:35 (NIV)

"Do nothing out of selfish ambition or vain conceit. Rather, in humility value others above yourselves… In your relationships with one another, have the same mindset as Christ Jesus." (Philippians 2:3–5 NIV)

Self-Sacrifice

"Then He said to them all: 'Whoever wants to be my disciple must deny themselves and take up their cross daily and follow me.'" (Luke 9:23 NIV)

Love

"Love the Lord your God with all your heart…' This is the first and greatest commandment. And the second is like it: 'Love your neighbor as yourself.'" (Matthew 22:37–39 NIV)

Seek God

"But seek first the kingdom of God and his righteousness, and all these things will be added to you" (Matthew 6:33 ESV)

"And without faith it is impossible to please
God… He rewards those who earnestly seek him."
(Hebrews 11:6 NIV)

Pure Heart

"Man looks at the outward appearance, but the
LORD looks at the heart." (1 Samuel 16:7 ESV)

"Blessed are the pure in heart, for they will see
God." (Matthew 5:8 NIV)

Caring for the Vulnerable

"Religion that God our Father accepts as pure and
faultless is this: to look after orphans and widows
in their distress." (James 1:27 NIV)

He has shown you, O man, what is good; and
what does the LORD require of you but to do
justice, to love mercy, and to walk humbly with
your God?" (Micah 6:8 NKJV)

These are just a few criteria on God's measuring stick of
greatness. I encourage you to continue your own list as you open
the Bible and read his Word. When you align your life, your
purpose, and your heart with His measuring stick, the fruit that
will be produced is far greater than anything you could have
imagined. Why? Because His fruit is supernatural and His
promises are eternal!

So go ahead and take some time to ask God to realign your goals, dreams, and visions for success with His and watch God do the impossible in your life.

Journal Time

What have you been using as a measuring stick for success?

What is one Scripture you can focus on that will help align your measurement of greatness with God's true measuring stick?

Confess + Connect with Jesus

Day 20

When Emotions Get the Best of You

Sometimes I let my emotions get the best of me. A very close friend of mine has a tough time controlling her emotions. Competition brings out her best and worst. It's like she gets tunnel vision and gets so wrapped up in the moment she cannot take a step back and breathe. She rides or dies on every play. Each point is a mini victory, and each error is like someone just stabbed her in the back. Maybe I'm exaggerating just a bit, but you get the point. You might even know someone like my good friend.

The Bible talks a lot about emotions:

> "Then Jesus wept [at Lazarus' death]." (John 11:35)

> "He looked around at them angrily and was deeply saddened by their hard hearts." (Mark 3:5)

"The Lord is close to the brokenhearted; he rescues those whose spirits are crushed." (Psalm 34:18)

God created emotion. Feelings and emotions are not a bad thing. But how do we respond when we are overcome with emotions? You see Jesus had emotions but never sinned. Our perfect example! We cannot get caught up in labeling emotions as bad because God created us with feelings. He also created us with a free will. We are not bound to being led or overcome by our emotions. We don't have to respond negatively to our anger or resentment or hurt, causing us to sin, but we can allow our emotions to lead us to our Savior.

"Whoever is patient has great understanding, but one who is quick-tempered displays folly." (Proverbs 14:29 NIV)

"But the fruit of the Spirit is love, joy, peace, patience, kindness, goodness, faithfulness, gentleness and self-control." (Galatians 5:22–23 NIV)

"Everyone should be quick to listen, slow to speak and slow to become angry, because human anger does not produce the righteousness that God desires." (James 1:19–20 NIV)

We are reminded in Scripture that the Holy Spirit gives us strength to overcome sinful desires. Our feelings should draw us closer to God. He cares for us! He wants to sit with you in your deepest pain. Your frustrations matter to Him. You should "cast your cares on Him for he cares for you" (1 Peter 5:7 NIV).

Present your emotions to God and let His Spirit fill you with His fruit: joy, peace, patience, gentleness, and self-control. Now I will admit, self-control and patience are hard ones. I'm still praying God gives me more of those fruits in my life. But by His grace, He is walking with me and feeling every emotion that I do, and He longs to fill me up with His Holy Spirit who gives me supernatural power to overcome sin and truly walk in freedom.

Journal Time

When do you find yourself unable to control your emotions?

God gave you your emotions when you were born. How can your emotions point you to Jesus?

Confess + Connect with Jesus

Day 21

Let the Big Dogs Eat

"I'm *starving!* I could eat a whole pizza!"

I've said this before. I hate getting to the point where my tummy grumbles and rumbles, and I feel light-headed. It's not a feeling we like to feel repeatedly. I almost always find myself overbuying food in the grocery store if I shop when I'm hungry.

But really, do you eat more when you're starving? Some might disagree.

In a world where it just makes sense to eat when you're starving and not eat when you're full let me challenge your mind to think outside the box.

Fact: Eating will make you want to eat more!

Think about your game. When you win, doesn't it feel good? Does it make you want to go out there and find another team to take down because you are on a roll? When you play a rival opponent, there's nothing sweeter than coming out victorious.

Winning is contagious! You tasted it and now you want more of it! In the same way, feeding your spirit the Word of God will create a deeper hunger to read it more.

> "People do not live by bread alone,
> but by every word that comes from the mouth of
> God." (Matthew 4:4)

> "Your words were found, and I ate them, and your
> words became to me a joy and the delight of my
> heart, for I am called by your name, O LORD, God of
> hosts." (Jeremiah 15:16 ESV)

Just like we feed our bodies to remain alive, the Bible tells us that we need to feed our spirit the Word of God. Are you feeding your spirit what it needs or is your spirit suffering from a lack of nutrients?

If you struggle with finding time to open the Bible, there are many helpful apps you can download and read the Bible on the go, such as YouVersion, Bible Gateway, or Blue Letter Bible. There's even features on some apps where you can listen to scripture on audio. You can be walking across campus, waiting in line, or even sitting on the team bus on your way to a game and be fed spiritually.

Whatever is the best way for you to receive the Word of God, get it in your spirit *today*! Stop starving yourself of spiritual nutrition. Now you know that your body *and* spirit need food, what are you going to do about it?

Once you taste the goodness of God and read His love letters to you, a deeper desire and hunger will grow. You will never want to starve again!

Just like winning is contagious, feast on Jesus's words for you when you open the Bible each day. Allow His Word to become your spiritual bread, and He will nourish you in far better ways than you could ever imagine.

Let the big dogs eat!

Journal Time

When or where do you find the best time to spend with God?

Have you ever felt spiritually filled up or maybe spiritually dry? What were your habits like during each of those times?

Confess + Connect with Jesus

Day 22

"Help, I'm About to Snap!"

I find myself at my wit's end when I feel out of control. Either life is just closing in on me, or the demands and responsibilities are simply overwhelming. I teeter between feeling okay and flipping a switch. Have you ever been there?

Girl, I am sitting in the middle of it right now as I write. Consider this a journal entry today more than an "I have it all together" devotional. I am speaking from the middle of my mess, and I just had to find a quiet space to write.

I need the Lord always. But at this moment, I need him *and* all the fruit of the Spirit: patience, peace, self-control, and love. Days just unfold before us, and sometimes nothing goes our way. People react, behaviors are irrational, and it's like you can't catch a break. Do I hear an amen? Everything in me is screaming to react in my flesh. I want to flip out, I want to run, I want to find anything that calms me down in the heat of the moment.

I need to remind myself that this too shall pass. In the middle of my emotional storm, I can either let the storm fester and grow, or I can be reminded that the wind of the Holy Spirit blows all storms to pass. I just need to heed God's words: "Be still and know that I am God! I will be exalted among the nations. I will be exalted in the earth" (Psalm 46:10).

I'm learning that just because my environment around me is chaos, I do not have to be a mirror reflection of that. I can respond with clarity and self-control when I keep my eyes focused on Him.

This is a two-part reminder:

1. Keep your eyes focused on Him, not on the circumstance.
2. Get filled up before you pour out.

Part two is critical before you ever start your day. I must be filled with his Spirit and His Word before I do anything! So often I wake up and grab my coffee hoping it will fill me up, but caffeine can only go so far before I have a mental crash halfway through the day. When we are filled with the Holy Spirit, we overflow as we keep our eyes fixed on Jesus! Our faith grows, our minds are at rest, and our hearts are safe. I can live out of *that* love every day of my life!

So today, I choose to be still in His holy presence. I will pray and ask God for His Spirit to fill me, supernaturally. Because I want to walk out of this room with my cup abundantly full so that I can give the love of Jesus to others amid all the chaos that life brings!

"But the fruit of the Spirit is love, joy, peace, forebearance, kindness, goodness, faithfulness, gentleness and self-control. Against such things there is no law."
— *Galatians 5:22–23 NIV*

Journal Time

What do you run to or how do you naturally respond when life just feels overwhelming?

How can you acknowledge your emotions and remain calm in the storm of the moment?

Confess + Connect with Jesus

Day 23

Drowning in Demands

Call it pressure, stress, paralysis. Whatever it is, we are overwhelmed.

Sometimes I think the word *overwhelmed* is under appreciated. This word has so many emotions that sum up how we feel. Whatever they are, it is overwhelming us. When I picture this word in my head, I get an image of a tidal wave washing over my entire body. Not in a good way like a cleansing refreshment. I'm talking loud, crashing, enormously strong and heavy weight of water dumping on top of me, swallowing me up and pulling me under. I have nothing to stand on, no help to hold on to.

When I am overwhelmed, I panic, just like Peter.

Peter, one of Jesus' closest disciples, felt overwhelmed.

In Matthew 14, the disciples were caught in a storm on the lake. Jesus appeared walking on water toward them. Amazed and frightened, they thought he was a ghost, but Jesus assured them it was Him. Peter wanted to go a step further and said, 'Lord, if it's really you, tell me to come to you" (Matthew 14:28). A miracle in itself, Jesus said, "Come" and Peter stepped out of the boat and started walking on water toward Jesus.

"But when he saw the strong wind and the waves, he was terrified and began to sink. "Save me, Lord!" he shouted" (Matthew 14:30)

What happened?

Focus. When we take our eyes off the Savior, we lose it and we panic! Look at Peter. He was walking on water when he kept his gaze locked on Jesus. But the moment he looked around him, he panicked and began to drown.

Life has a funny way of distracting our hearts and minds to think of everything but the One who holds our lives in his hands. When we shift our focus to the things here on Earth, we get consumed (and even stressed) by all the emotions that flood our hearts. It's as if the world is caving in, a tidal wave overwhelms our thoughts! Our bodies physically react to stress. The stress hormones cortisol and adrenaline increase. Your heart starts beating rapidly. You sweat. The fight-flight-or-freeze response kicks in. You can feel the blood rush through your entire body. Muscle tension. Maybe even digestive issues!

Long-term stress in your body is debilitating. It weakens your immune system, making you more susceptible to sickness. It can lead to irregular sleep or lack of sleep, health problems, and more! Do you see how our mind and body are interconnected?

In the middle of feeling overwhelmed, sometimes all we need to do is look up. Regain our focus on the Savior and stop looking at the winds and the waves crashing over us. Jesus doesn't promise the problems of life will go away, but He promises to be with you through it all. You will make it through. Take care of your body by renewing your mind. You have all that you need, and it is found in Jesus!

So if you are feeling a little overwhelmed by all that life throws your way, remember to look up! Refocus and open your heart for Him to fill with you with His peace that passes all understanding today!

Journal Time

What stressors are you dealing with today?

How does your body respond to stress? Pay attention to the physical response your body gives you when you start to feel these emotions take over.

Confess + Connect with Jesus

Day 24

Self-Check!

How are you doing?

I don't ask this question like a barista asks a customer before taking your order at the drive thru. I'm asking you this question like a true friend who sees there is something deeper going on in your heart. Consider taking some time to spend on this devotion today.

If you don't quite know how to respond to the question: "How is your heart doing?" Consider starting here:

- Do circumstances or people get under your skin?
- Are you frustrated in this season of your life?
- Do you have emotions that are too big to handle sometimes?
- Do peace, love, and self-control sound like a foreign language to you?
- Are you disappointed?
- Do you have unmet expectations?

- Is your heart at rest or unsettled?
- Are you doubtful/fearful or does worry overtake you?
- Are you just unsure of yourself?
- Do you second guess a lot?

If you answered yes to any of these questions, rest easy, my friend. You are not alone! Fear, doubt, stress, anxiety, overthinking, and disappointment are all *real* and can show up in our lives often without us even noticing what they are or what they can do to you.

You might be wondering, "What do you mean by 'what they can do to you'?" When you are overwhelmed by these feelings, it can lead you to anger, resentment, jealousy, bitterness, lust, and gluttony.

Yuck! Those responses sound evil. Who would admit to these ugly things?

But this was me, or this can *still* be me, to this day!

When I get overwhelmed by all the hats I wear each day (mom, wife, mentor, teacher, diaper changer, chef, uber driver, coach, business owner, house cleaner, teammate, and personal bank) sometimes it can be overwhelming. And when I get pushed to my limit, I break. Call it rage. Yes, I'm angry. Frustrated. Mad. Tired. Exhausted. All the above. I can very easily run to food or coffee or ice cream as a coping mechanism. Or worse, I might start doom scrolling on social media to numb the pain. I can be mad at my husband for not helping me juggle a million things while he gets to go to the gym every day and complete his do-to list for work. I'm bitter. He's better. Meanwhile, my hair is on fire. And I am hangry.

Did you see how quickly one day can spiral for me? I went from being overwhelmed to bitterness, rage, and jealousy. One thing they all have in common: sin. God calls this sin.

> "Everyone should be quick to listen, slow to speak and slow to become angry, because human anger does not produce the righteousness that God desires." (James 1:19–20 NIV)

> "Fools give full vent to their rage, but the wise bring calm in the end." (Proverbs 29:11 NIV)

> "In your anger do not sin": Do not let the sun go down while you are still angry, and do not give the devil a foothold." (Ephesians 4:26–27 NIV)

> "But now you must also rid yourselves of all such things as these: anger, rage, malice." (Colossians 3:8 NIV)

> "For where you have envy and selfish ambition, there you find disorder and every evil practice." (James 3:16 NIV)

Do you see how my heart is not okay? It is so incredibly important to do heart checks often. Why? Because sin will creep in before we even realize it. The Enemy wants us to live in fear, doubt, anxiety, and frustration. The more we let it go unchecked, the easier we are to fall into temptation and sin. The ugly sin. But here's the good news. We can become clean!

"Create in me a clean heart, O God. Renew a loyal spirit within me. Do not banish me from your presence, and don't take your Holy Spirit from me. Restore to me the joy of your salvation and make me willing to obey you."
— *Psalm 51:10–12*

What do you run to when you need to cool off?

If your heart is feeling much like mine, take a moment and pray and ask God to reveal the sin that sits underneath these emotions that seem overwhelming. List them here.

Confess + Connect with Jesus

Day 25

Three Keys to the Next Level

1. Show Up

Consistency is powerful! Whatever you can give, show up each and every day. Would you want a friend who is there for you only when it's convenient for them? Or do you appreciate the faithfulness of a loyal friend through thick and thin?

Even when days are less than glamorous for you—you're tired, exhausted, stressed, hangry, sore, or just not feeling it—are you able to drag yourself out of bed and onto the field? Can you give your mind a little pep talk before you step on to the court or gym? Remind yourself to just show up! I am so thankful that God always is there for me. He never takes a day off; He is faithful to his children, and I know I can always count on him.

The Lord blesses those who continually show up, who are faithful, and never give up. Remember, God will give you the strength you need if you ask.

"Therefore, my beloved brothers, be steadfast, immovable, always abounding in the work of the Lord, knowing that in the Lord your labor is not in vain." (1 Corinthians 15:58 ESV)

"And let us not grow weary of doing good, for in due season we will reap, if we do not give up." (Galatians 6:9 ESV)

2. Take Ownership

Remember that God has called us to walk our own faith journey with Him. Our path is not our family's path. They cannot make the decisions for you. Our relationship with our heavenly Father is precious and unique. He speaks directly to you!

When faced with challenges in your path, you can either run from them or face them. This requires taking ownership. No excuses! No blaming! Own your decisions, the outcome, the consequences, and the lessons learned. You will be a better woman by accepting these head on. The faster you can learn this crucial key, the quicker you will see yourself flourish.

God can speak through tough moments in your life. You are not alone.

"Pay careful attention to your own work, for then you will get the satisfaction of a job well done, and you won't need to compare yourself to anyone else. For we are each responsible for our own conduct." (Galatians 6:4-5)

3. Never Stop Learning

I did not enjoy studying for tests in high school and college. I would rather do worksheets, homework, or write a paper any day of the week! When it came to quizzes and finals, I was stressed! Why? Because tests and quizzes revealed my comprehension and retention of what I learned. I had to apply my knowledge to get a good grade. It had to sink in! I would much rather fill out a worksheet that requires zero thinking skills while getting to peek at an open textbook the entire time.

But life is full of tests that require you to respond based on the knowledge you've attained. There's no cheating in the moment! No shortcuts, no take-home quizzes. Whatever you have learned up until this point will help you navigate your decisions through it. So, my question to you is this: What are you learning so that you will have even greater tools to use when life throws you a curveball?

I love podcasts. They're easy for me to digest when I am on the go. But nothing beats my quiet time where I can sit in my comfy chair where I find peace and time to be still. My brain slows down. I can focus on being in the moment, and I have time to gather my thoughts and ponder all the blessings God has already given me. Nothing fills my cup spiritually more than reading the Bible. God's Word gets planted in my heart, and I know I am planting good seeds in the soil of my life when I create space for Him. The Bible has a lot to say about learning and wisdom and knowledge. Consider these verses:

> "For the LORD gives wisdom; from his mouth come knowledge and understanding." (Proverbs 2:6)

> "The heart of the discerning acquires knowledge, for the ears of the wise seek it out." (Proverbs 18:15 NIV)

> "The fear of the Lord is the beginning of knowledge, but fools despise wisdom and instruction." (Proverbs 1:7 NIV)

> "If any of you lacks wisdom, let him ask of God, who gives to all liberally and without reproach, and it will be given to him." (James 1:5 NKJV)

> "And this is my prayer: that your love may abound more and more in knowledge and depth of insight." (Philippians 1:9 NIV)

Be a life-long learner! There is always something new to learn!

Journal Time

What are some new ways that you can grow in your spiritual life? In your sport?

What areas of your life do you want to grow in taking ownership?

Confess + Connect with Jesus

Day 26

No Excuses

When I was younger, I got in trouble with my parents and teachers at school. I would immediately begin to make excuses for what happened. Someone else made me do it. That person started it. Or I acted clueless like I didn't know what I was doing.

Bottom line: it wasn't my fault.

The older I got, the more I realized I wasn't fooling anyone. They could see right through my lies and excuses, and there was no one to blame but myself. I know that excuses don't make me look better. They just make it look like I can't handle my own choices.

Ouch!

There was a man in the Bible who blamed someone else for his own sin: Adam. The first man God ever created on Earth. God told him not to eat from one particular tree, but he could eat everything else in the garden. When God found Adam and Eve hiding in the bushes one day, He asked them why they were hiding. They said they were ashamed because they were naked. And then God said, "'Who told you that you were naked? Have you eaten from the tree that I commanded you not to eat from?' The man said, 'The woman you put here with me—she gave me some fruit from the tree, and I ate it'" (Genesis 3:11–12 NIV)

Blame-shifting is a real thing and it's easy to do. We do it because we don't want to look bad to others, but in reality, we look even worse when we can't confess to our own mistakes and choices. The bottom line is we don't want to take responsibility for our own actions. We don't want to reap the consequences of our poor behavior.

Let's take a look at one more popular man in the Bible: Aaron. He was Moses's brother and helper in freeing the Israelites from slavery in Egypt. There were over a million of them—what a huge task! In the middle of leading these people to freedom, Moses goes to the top of a mountain to talk to God. He was gone for forty days. The people were upset because they were stuck in the desert. The Israelite people persuaded Aaron to build a golden calf to worship. Aaron gave in to the pressure and to appease them he made the idol. Later, when Moses came down the mountain from receiving the Ten Commandments from God, Moses questioned Aaron about the idol in their camp. " 'Don't get so upset, my lord," Aaron replied. "You yourself know how evil these people are. They said to me, 'Make us gods who will lead us. We don't know what happened to this fellow Moses, who brought us here from the land of Egypt.' So I told them, 'Whoever has gold jewelry, take it off.' When they brought it to me, I simply threw it into the fire—and out came this calf!' " (Exodus 32:21–24).

What a lame excuse! Aaron was persuaded and allowed this golden calf to be made. Clearly, Aaron did not want to take responsibility for his actions and shifted the blame towards the Israelites.

Every now and then I will catch myself making up excuses in my head. I'm late because my kids wouldn't get it together. I rolled through that stop sign because I was late and no one was at the four-way stop. I was short with my husband when he came home from work because I had a hard day. I can cut my workout short by a few minutes because I'm just over this. Can you relate?

My self-talk is even making excuses! We are all prone to sin. We mess up. We make mistakes. But here is where the Enemy will try to keep you in sin: blame-shifting! He whispers to you that you're not wrong. You were only reacting to the people around you. It's not your fault! You are the helpless one. You are the one who was caught in the middle, and you can't be the one to blame.

We might think that if we take ownership of our own mistakes, then other people get a free pass because we are taking the fall for them. But that is not true! When we take responsibility for our own behavior, we show God and others that we are honest. The Bible says that "whoever conceals their sins does not prosper, but the one who confesses and renounces them finds mercy" (Proverbs 28:13 NIV). We need to own up to our actions. God is pleased when he sees his children learning and growing in righteousness, walking in His ways. He says, "I have taught you the way of wisdom; I have led you in the paths of uprightness. When you walk, your step will not be hampered" (Proverbs 4:11–12 ESV). He will give you the courage and strength you need to resist blaming others and stop making excuses. Choose to walk in freedom!

No excuses!

Journal Time

How are you just like Adam and Aaron?

How will taking responsibility for your actions this week help you become a better woman and athlete?

Confess + Connect with Jesus

Day 27

Two Must-Haves for Every Female Athlete

1. A Good Sports Bra

You might laugh at the thought of this being a top finisher on my list, but hear me out.

When you are picking out a sports bra for practice do you constantly look for a certain one in your drawer? Yup! That's *the* one! Your eyes search for it among the many you own. Why? Because it fits just right. It could be the way it feels. The material is light and breathable, it's easy to put on, and it's supportive in every sense of the word.

There are certain criteria every female athlete has for their sports bras. It must be comfortable and sized correctly. There's nothing worse than having to wear a tight and restrictive bra when you are constantly moving at practice. So uncomfortable!

It also must be moisture-wicking, down to the small details: holes, breathable, good material. We do not want to sweat and keep that sweat inside our clothes for hours. Yuck! The function of a sports bra must move moisture away from your body and not trap it all day, right?!

And lastly, it must be supportive. The material should be made of quality fabric that is guaranteed to hold us through the most intense workouts.

Sports bras were created for athletes like you and me! We can appreciate the craftsmanship of the sports bra and will pay a pretty penny because it's worth it. Just go one day without it and you will feel the difference! Everyone knows the feeling of forgetting your sports bra at home at least once and having to suffer through an entire practice or game with a regular bra. Ugh!

If you came up to me and asked, "how should I live my best life?" I would tell you to live like your favorite sports bra: don't be so uptight, breathe a little, don't hold stuff in. Let the stinky stuff wick right off you, and don't forget to always be supportive to your friends, family, and teammates!

2. Encouraging and Uplifting Playlist

I love music! If it's a good beat and uplifting words, I'm sold. Put it on my playlist. I've learned over the years that good beats aren't the end-all to choosing what I listen to. As I've gotten older, I've really started to pay attention to what the artist is saying. There is always a message hidden between the bars. I've learned to focus on this because whatever I allow in my ears goes straight to my heart. Like a sticker, it's stuck to my heart.

The Bible explains the importance of guarding what we put into our minds and focusing on what is true and encouraging. Consider the following verses:

> "Finally, brothers and sisters, whatever is true, whatever is noble, whatever is right, whatever is pure, whatever is lovely, whatever is admirable—if anything is excellent or praiseworthy—think about such things." (Philippians 4:8 NIV)

> "Gracious words are a honeycomb, sweet to the soul and healing to the bones." (Proverbs 16:24 NIV)

> "I have hidden your word in my heart that I might not sin against you." (Psalm 119:11 NIV)

> "My son, pay attention to what I say; turn your ear to my words. Do not let them out of your sight, keep them within your heart; for they are life to those who find them and health to one's whole body. Above all else, guard your heart, for everything you do flows from it." (Proverbs 4:20–23 NIV)

Life forces us to rush things, to make split decisions, to not think too deeply about things, and then move on. Look, life is too stressful as it is! How are you filling your cup and heart that puts you in a good mood and positive mindset? It's easy to brush this off and choose music with a good vibe and less than encouraging lyrics. But oh, my friend, how is your heart doing? Is life full of chaos, anger, fear, selfishness, bitterness, anxiety, and loneliness? Add some encouraging music to your playlist each day. Let the words wash over you and fill you up! When I'm in a stressed-out mood, I look forward to my uplifting songs that will be stuck in my head for the rest of the day.

Encouraging music refocuses my brain on the things of heaven with eternal perspective. My mood shifts; I feel God's peace and presence with me whenever I listen to good music.

Journal Time

What are a few must-haves that are already a part of your daily life and how do they help you?

Is there anything that you need to get rid of or add to your list?

Confess + Connect with Jesus

Day 28

Stronger in the Shift

We all have similar journeys in life. We may find ourselves stuck or just in a place where we don't want to be for a long period of time. We have dreams, visions, goals, and aspirations. We want to create a life that is successful and satisfying in our own eyes. We want to get this life up off the ground and soar.

We are here, and we want to get there—wherever there is. I can help you!

Pro tip: get comfortable with transitions!

I know you want to get there, but you cannot bypass the journey. The quicker you can recognize and navigate transitions, the easier the journey will become. I've heard it said that life is just a series of transitions. You're either going into one, in the middle of one, or coming out of one. That phrase has stuck with me for a very long time. We must learn to sit in the uncomfortableness of life sometimes. We cannot always solve our way out of a season of life. Sometimes we were meant to sit in it and learn. It's uncomfortable, it may be annoying or downright unfair. But identify it as a transition. You're on your way to *there*.

Let's look at Joseph in the Bible. He was the youngest of eleven sons of Jacob. The baby of them all. On top of that Joseph's dad gave him a robe, beautifully decorated as a symbol of his father's love. God gave Joseph a dream that he would rule over his brothers and even his parents one day! Young Joseph blabbed this dream to his older brothers. Can you imagine how jealous they were towards Joseph?

They decided to just throw him in a pit and leave him there to die. But his oldest brother had a better idea. They sold him into slavery.

What a life! Joseph has this high calling from God, and his own flesh and blood wanted him dead. If you have ever felt like your life is the pits, think how bad Joseph had it.

Joseph's life got a little better when he was owned by Potiphar, a captain of the guard, who trusted Joseph to run his whole household. Well, that didn't last long because Potiphar's wife lied and accused Joseph of coming on to her. Potiphar had Joseph arrested.

Back to the pits!

Years later, he was released from prison. God did not forget about him or his promise to Joseph!

Eventually, Joseph became ruler over all of Egypt and the story came full circle when his brothers traveled to Egypt begging for food during a famine. Joseph had compassion over his brothers and God used Joseph mightily to save Egypt from starvation.

From the pits to the palace!

Joseph faced dramatic transitions throughout his life. But he remained faithful to God and was a light to the world at each transition he faced. He could've easily quit, had a bad attitude, and given up on God's promise. But he was steadfast in every season of his life. He impacted so many along the way, and I believe that is what truly built Joseph for his ultimate seat in the palace!

Embrace change! See what job God is asking you do to in the transition. Keep the faith! Know that every chapter of your life either sharpens you, refines you, or blesses you! You are well on your way to the palace!

"Be strong, and let your heart take courage, all you who wait for the LORD."
— Psalm 31:24 NIV

Journal Time

Are you in the middle of a transition, about to go into one, or just coming out of one?

How have you handled transitions in the past? How do you view these moments in your life?

Confess + Connect with Jesus

Day 29

When My Stats Don't Stack Up

The most important thing to remember as a female athlete: Your value is bigger than your stats!

Do you stress about stats, that little number next to your name when coaches and opponents scout you? Do you value this more than your actual name? As a college athlete, my answer was a resounding yes! But years later, my answer has changed.

You see, I lived and died by those numbers. If they were high, I would be okay. If they started dropping, I panicked. I was stressed. I was worried. I tried even harder to get back to where I thought I should be. But all it did was make me a frazzled mess, and I could feel myself obsessing about every little thing. I lost sight of the game and put all the pressure on my performance. There was no more *team*, but only *me*.

Can I encourage you today? Your worth is not found in numbers. Your worth is found inside you. When you read your name on that stat sheet, forget the numbers. Focus on your name. Why? Because when someone calls your name, they are calling who you are.

You are beautiful.

You are chosen.

You are priceless.

You are victorious.

You are kind.

You are compassionate.

You are smart.

You make others feel seen and loved.

You bring people joy.

The list can go on and on. Your stats say nothing about the core of you. You are worth so much more than numbers. Guess what? Those numbers can change at any moment. Don't hang on too tightly!

Remember, Christ died for you, not your stats. His love is boundless! He stepped in and took our place because he values and loves us as we are. The Bible speaks clearly about how God views you, His creation. Consider the following verses:

> "How precious are your thoughts about me, O God.
> They cannot be numbered! I can't even count them;

147

they outnumber the grains of sand! And when I wake up, you are still with me!" (Psalms 139:17–18)

"But now thus says the LORD, he who created you, O Jacob, he who formed you, O Israel: 'Fear not, for I have redeemed you; I have called you by name, you are mine.'" (Isaiah 43:1 ESV)

"See what kind of love the Father has given to us, that we should be called children of God; and so we are." (1 John 3:1 ESV)

So, the next time you are tempted to magnify those numbers, remember to focus on your name. You are worth more to your heavenly Father than anything else in this world. You can rest knowing He is proud of you no matter what anyone else sees!

Journal Time

Do you ever find yourself getting consumed by your stats in the middle of season? Why?

What is one practical way you can refocus on the truth of who God calls you as a female athlete?

Confess + Connect with Jesus

Day 30

The Secret to Being Content

It's not that I have everything I need. It's that the One who has everything I need is already in me.

Don't get me wrong. I'm no different than you. I have needs, wants, desires, and dreams. This constant desire to reach, attain, strive toward, and obtain is innate. Goals are not a bad thing.

And I'm not even talking about the American dream gone rogue (the idea that we are never satisfied with what we have, we always want more, what someone else has. That is a completely different topic of sin). No, this contentment is what I long for when I have a need that must be met. A bill that must be paid. A crisis that needs to be solved in my head so I can stop worrying. Have you come across a need that must be met this week?

Often, we don't even recognize our needs. We bypass the problem altogether as we launch straight into a response. We immediately let our God-given brain fly into options A, B, and

C. It's quite a beautiful thing to think about how our minds are built to solve problems.

But in between the *need* and *response* is what I am highlighting for you and me today. The realization that God meets all my needs, yes, I said *all*.

Sometimes I find it hard to believe this truth, but I can say it over and over again without hesitation. My head knows that God is my Provider, but do I really rely on Him when a need pops up, or do I try to lean on my own ways to figure this out? I know the Scripture says to trust in the Lord with all your heart...but do I always remember this command in between the need and the response? No.

When I choose my response without resting in Jesus as my Provider, I kick into fear, panic, stress, worry—all things that do not come from God. But when I can wrap my head around Jesus holding my need in the palm of his hand and telling me it's going to be okay, I somehow have a peace that completely washes over me because deep down, my heart trusts Him.

I want that, every time!

Consider the words of the apostle Paul on the matter of trusting God and finding contentment in Him:

> "I know how to live on almost nothing or with
> everything. I have learned the secret of living in every

situation, whether it is with a full stomach or empty, with plenty or little. For I can do everything through Christ, who gives me strength." (Philippians 4:12-13)

"Don't worry about anything; instead, pray about everything. Tell God what you need and thank him for all he has done. Then you will experience God's peace, which exceeds anything we can understand. His peace will guard your hearts and minds as you live in Christ Jesus." (Philippians 4:6-7)

It's comforting to see all throughout Scripture this truth that God provides and truly meets all our needs. He already supplies the answer, we just need to trust that He has made a way!

In the beginning God created the heavens and the Earth. He created air for us to breathe before He even created humans. He already met our needs before man ever came onto the scene. God didn't create lungs in Adam and Eve and then realize they needed air to breathe—quite the opposite. He created air before he created humans. The answer was already in existence before there was a need or problem.

Doesn't that put your heart at ease? God is omniscient—all knowing. He is omnipotent—all powerful, able to do anything. He is omnipresent. He is everywhere at the same time. Nothing is too big for our God! We can exhale and give our worries to

Him. In between the need and the answer, I pray you will remember the magnitude of our great Father! He is the one we run to first. This is the lesson of finding contentment in all things.

"And this same God who takes care of me will supply all your needs from his glorious riches, which have been given to us in Christ Jesus."

— Philippians 4:19

Journal Time

Are you a habitual worrier? What do you do when you find stress or anxiousness creep over you quickly?

Which verse speaks to your heart the loudest when you have unrest? Ask God to help you find contentment in Him when you need answers.

Confess + Connect with Jesus

Conclusion

Now that you have completed the thirty-day devotional, I pray this one theme resonates: that you are victorious in Christ Jesus. You can do all things through Christ who gives you strength (Philippians 4:13)! If you have accepted Jesus as your Lord and Savior, you are on God's team. If you have not surrendered your life to Christ, I would be honored to walk you through a simple prayer. Romans 10:13 says "everyone who calls on the name of the Lord will be saved." If you want the gift of eternal salvation, pray this prayer with me:

Dear Jesus, please forgive me of my sins. I know I am not perfect and I fall short of God's glory. I need a Savior. I ask you to come into my heart and I surrender to your will. I choose you as Lord of my life. I believe you are the risen Savior. You died on the cross for my sins and rose from the grave. So today, I confess with my mouth that you are my Lord and Savior, I place my faith in you alone. Thank you for giving me the free gift of eternal life. I choose to walk in freedom from this moment forward. I am no longer bound to sin. In Jesus name, amen!

Welcome to the family! I pray this devotional is one you can read over and over again in all seasons of life, long after sports are gone. Pass along this book to a young athlete who needs to be reminded that she is victorious, too!

www.ingramcontent.com/pod-product-compliance
Lightning Source LLC
Chambersburg PA
CBHW020356130626
46549CB00006B/2297